# My Pocketbook of
# I Love You's

**Author: Madeline Rose Fiore**

Illustrations by Vikki Mera

*Copyright © 2019 by Madeline Rose Fiore*

@oh_madeline_

Love is complex. There is no perfect way to do anything. Some people are great lovers, others have no idea how to love. They say love can be easy, but for those who endured a more one-sided love, or a love based out of fear, or even a love that fills a void, we all know that love isn't easy. We're supposed to trust our instincts, but sometimes our hearts disagree with our gut. Our hearts can be pumping for what our mind is telling us is no good. We sit here envisioning ways to make it all better but forget that our mind fails to run parallel with reality.

When it comes to disagreements, we fail to recognize that the people around us may not actually react the way we envisioned. I guess we truly don't know what good, healthy love is until we are in it. I've witnessed many different kinds of love and still doubt that true love exists. We can connect with someone, but does that truly mean we are meant to be with them?

There are so many questions I wish I had the answers to, but when the time is meant for me to find out, I will. Here is my side of one type of love I've endured…

"Sometimes when you're in the dark, you ignore the light. Look again, let it in, now begin…" - Madeline Rose Fiore

@oh_madeline_

HONEYMOON

**Hello My Light**

So maybe if the wind didn't blow,
Would your light shine into my life?

There is a sky full of stars,
But only one stands out,
Where did all the other ones go?

As I move closer to this one of a kind,
All that went wrong declutters my mind.

You don't know the impact you have,
For when I close my eyes there you are again.

I absorb you like the grass does with water on a hot summer day,
I breathe you in like you're the only oxygen my lungs can take.

There is a world surrounding us ready to explore,
Don't think for a second you are not the one I adore.

Your name is on my lips,
Waiting to become permanent.

Take my hand,
I know it seems scary,
But there is a light at the end of my tunnel...

One that shines as bright as yours.

@oh_madeline_

**08/15/18**

    I turn over in my sleep to hold the love of my life, I never knew how beautiful someone could feel in my arms. She makes my heart melt. It's a warm feeling I've never felt. I've been told before that I was someone's person, but never thought I'd find *my* person. Here she is, laying beside me, she sleeps so peacefully. Her eyelashes move slowly with the pace of her breathing, she smirks every time I move in closer.

Loving you is like finally breaking into a lighthouse and admiring the view.

**Can I Come In?**

I've acquired a love I truly desire,
It rotates me faster than a tire.

Off she goes with my heart,
I'm so glad I hit restart.

I wanted to isolate,
But she is my soulmate.

I remember looking into her eyes when she was not mine,
Oh how I wanted our souls to intertwine.

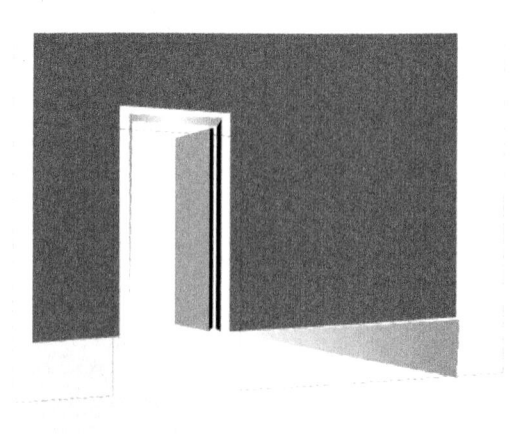

**08/17/18**

    Sometimes you need a voice to tell you that you're going nowhere. I used to let that voice take over my mind and lead me into a dark tunnel. Now that I've found the light, she pulls me up and shows me that it's all going to be alright. She reminds me that I am going to get there. She saved me when I needed saving. Every day she holds me close and every time I look into her eyes I see how bright they sparkle. She admires me in a way I've never been admired before. She pushes me to keep going. She's someone I've never had and someone I'll never meet again. She's one in a million. It's odd, the way the universe works. Once one toxic figure leaves, the rest will follow. All the empty faces will disappear because she will be the one that outshines them all.

@oh_madeline_

I looked at every cloud and wondered which one would make you think of me.

**I See You Are My Sun**

I've swiped this earth,
Looking for a soul that comes from new birth.

My sweet sun,
You are the most fun.

I forgot what it's like to breathe,
I promise I will never leave.

I've made a fool of myself,
But please don't keep me on your shelf.

I want to see,
All that we can be.

@oh_madeline_

**08/20/18**

    I keep having dreams where everyone else turns into you. I guess the reality is that you're always on my mind, even when I'm sleeping. I'd rather spend my time with you.

I used to climb every tree I saw
because I wanted to
see the different views.

**Here Come The Changes**

The changes keep coming,
I wish for more funding,

I know I can make it,
But I've fallen into a pit.

Two soft hands pull me up,
I'm no longer forced to drink from a cup.

**08/23/18**

    I don't want a time limit with you. I've already expressed that you're my 'forever'. I hadn't lived until I started living with you. You've moved into my life, made changes, and now I hope that you stay. I remember you asked me for forever when we first met. I never believed in something so everlasting, but you've changed that mindset. I'm not the best when it comes to expressing how I feel, so I'll write you a million poems. You are my forever, and there is no one better.

@oh_madeline_

save me

If I ever fell far enough,
would you notice and come
save me?

save me

## **Where Have You Been?**

You sunk with him,
I sunk with her.

You broke free,
And swam to me.

What took so long,
When all was going wrong?

I'm glad you came,
Our love won't go to shame.

@oh_madeline_

**08/27/18**

    I'd like to think I'm a very open person. I say things how they are, but I also know when to bite my tongue. I like to make others feel comfortable, so I talk a lot, I guess when no ones around to listen, I write. My life has changed a lot, but **the only constant thing in life is change.** She's the best change that's ever happened.

The sun beaming down on our skin is where I think we should begin.

**I Know I'm A Mess**

We met on a rocky start,
I know I broke your heart.

I've never felt this way before,
But I knew you were sure.

I kept bumping into you,
I know you wanted me too.

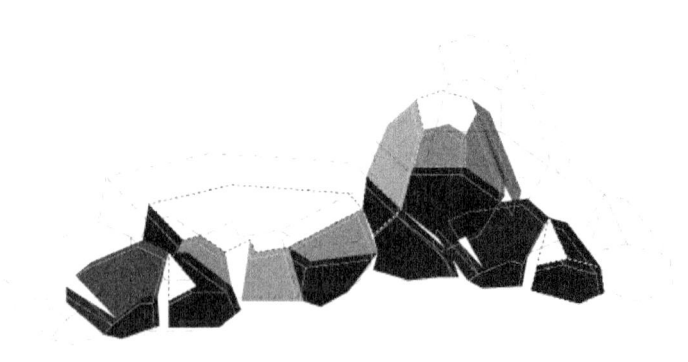

**08/30/18**

  Even in the most uncomfortable setting, she makes me feel safe. She has opened the door to a world of emotions hidden in my soul, we travel through it and hope to explore. She has a young mind and a scared heart. She is only her most fearless when by my side. She's ready for an adventure, an open spirit journey. Off I go with her, as I hope to do for the rest of our days.

  Wherever you wish to go, I will follow, your beauty inspires me and I'd be a fool to let you go.

  I will watch her explore the unknown and leave fragments of her soul in each place she steps. We all need to constantly find ourselves, she chooses to do so in the strangest of places.

  Together we embark on a new milestone in our relationship, we will continue to show our love for one another in a place as beautiful as our hearts. We are pure, we are gold, and we will continue to shine even in the darkness of the unknown.

@oh_madeline_

Good things always come into our lives,
it's just a matter of keeping it.

**All My Dreams Are About You**

Dim lights,
But everything seems too bright.

I guess that's what I mean,
When I tell you, you're a dream.

Darkness made me lose sight,
Here you are, my shining light.

I can't believe all that I see,
You're my favourite mystery.

@oh_madeline_

**09/10/18**

Where do your thoughts wander off to in a time of change? Some may think positive and others may not even notice what's changing. For those who are like myself, well you probably isolate yourself in darkness.

"You're so dark..." has to be one of my favourite sayings because it is something I have been told countless times. Is it odd that it sends soothing shivers down my spine?

It is like I admire that part of myself. Mostly because my darkest thoughts speak the loudest.

They fall in love with a writer until
the writer begins to write about them.

**Y O U**

I've ran into others,
I've had many lovers.

You've stopped my world,
I've always been swirled.

Lets start our life,
With you as my wife.

**09/15/18**

    I get sad easily. Instead of crying, I get angry. For some strange reason, I'd rather look "crazy" than reveal my true emotions. But that's just the cover of my book, until you open it up and read my pages. As I've grown, the people closest to me have been drifting. Instead of placing a bandaid over all their mistakes, I push them out of the door and lock it shut. I don't have time to be mistreated any more.

@oh_madeline_

I guess we all need to find
the one thing that keeps us sane,
no matter how insane it
actually might make us.

## I Love When You Touch Me

You unravel me,
You've made me your key.

I fit inside of you without too much pain,
I love when you scream my name.

You bite your lip,
I take a big sip.

@oh_madeline_

**09/20/18**

    I used to surround myself with so many nameless faces. I could never quite grasp how many people were beside me. I used to get anxious in crowded places, I still do. Eventually, all the friendly faces fade. We either push them away, or they go into hiding. The best are those who hide in plain sight. Most people become distant to improve themselves, (I would hope), I mean that's what I tend to do. Sometimes being surrounded by so many other people's thoughts and judgments block out your own. I haven't slept alone in months, and now I can't. There is only one person who can crowd my soul because she is my person. She's consumed me as a whole but has learned to let me go. We share a bed, like two people in love should.

Why can't every night
feel like the best night?

**Drowning For You**

I never realized how deep I was drowning.
Before you, I couldn't stop frowning.

She swam down to save me,
She refused to let me be.

I need her,
Like an animal needs their fur.

I didn't want to admit,
She wouldn't quit.

I float through this journey,
She keeps my world from burning.

**09/23/18**

    I was a *free spirit*. No one could stop me. At the same time, it felt like the world was holding me back. I'm used to a black and grey life, well of course, who isn't? Most people don't really feel their surroundings. Most people don't feel their emotions. My emotions and my feelings are what motivate me.

@oh_madeline_

I know right from wrong,
let's just move along.

**Read Me**

My sweet sun,
I've found you at last,
Let's begin our fun,
And move on from the past.

I feel your warmth on my skin,
When your hand is placed in mine,
I get lost when you kiss my chin,
There is no longer a need for time.

The dark clouds that once pulled me in,
I let my body absorb,
The earth has given me a chance to begin,
I put my life on do not disturb.

@oh_madeline_

**09/27/18**

    I swim to you as a child swims to their mother for safety. I finally know what it feels like to be held and adored. I know that when the waves rise to shore, you'll be there to save me. I admire you for your loving heart. You promised me the world and instead made me your world. I can't wait to keep on loving you, there are so many things I want to do.

Hold onto me,
there's still so much
to see.

**Give Me A Chance**

I've given myself a task,
When things get hard, just ask.

I've swam as far as I could,
I still felt misunderstood.

My journey is not over,
"My life is just beginning" is what I tell her.

**09/30/18**

    Through the highs and the lows, I've always been one to pull myself together. I guess I was never accepting of having someone else care for me, but now I have become so dependent on having you care for me. It's nice to have someone shower you with love in many different ways, but it's even better knowing it comes from you.

@oh_madeline_

I need another dose,
I desire you the most.

**Pack Your Bags**

Off we go,
We will never feel low.

A place of unknown,
Soon to feel like home.

She wants to be free,
But will never let me be.

I admire her smile,
I keep writing about her in a new file.

@oh_madeline_

**10/05/18**

    I replay the night we first met in my head. The nervous feeling, the excitement, it was such a rush. We know trouble would come from us being together, but we went about it anyways. You made me feel every emotion I could possibly feel at once. I was trying so hard to impress you, you were trying not to make too much eye contact with me. Then the kiss. That kiss sent me flying off into a whole new dimension. It felt so right, even while knowing it was completely wrong. I'm forever grateful for that night, I'm forever grateful to have met you, I know I can never forget you.

> Can you come over?

> Sure, I'm on my way!

> Okay, see you soon.

@oh_madeline_

**I'm Ready, Are You?**

Hold me back,
I will attack.

Kiss me slow,
Now it's time to go.

My soul is dark,
You're the only one who gives me a spark.

**10/08/18**

    I hate spending time away from you. I spend my time at work counting down the minutes until I can come home to you. My mind constantly replays the most beautiful images of you. I've never met a girl like you before. You came into my life so determined to get what you want and every day I see that smile on your face. I never thought I could make someone feel this happy to be with me. I hope the feeling doesn't fade, because I want you to stay.

@oh_madeline_

Another rainy day,
In my arms is where you lay.

**Thank You**

Standing up for myself was something
I could never do, until I met you.

I was easy to manipulate,
Until I met my soulmate.

The world wants to see me drown,
She wants to see me in a crown.

I know my true worth,
Now it's easier to roam this earth.

@oh_madeline_

**10/13/18**

Fuck,
I
love
you.

I truly forgot
what it was like
to live before
meeting you.

**My Majesty**

My beauty queen,
You're my wildest dream.

How could I have known,
That you would rule my thrown.

Our love cannot be dismissed,
It's your lips that are desired to be kissed.

My world continues to grow,
With you I never feel low.

Stay by my side,
I'll always wear you with pride.

**10/19/18**

    Waking up next to you is such an honour. I could never fall asleep at night and now I sleep so peacefully.

    I know I still talk in my sleep, but I hope I whisper beautiful words to you.

    I guess I talk in my sleep because I have so much to say, but there is so little time within a day.

@oh_madeline_

I say goodbye with a kiss.

## Shivers Down My Spine

The dark mornings get cold,
I need a coffee as strong as bold.

I chose my life the way I want,
Their evil words like to taunt.

She holds me close,
I can't get enough of her dose.

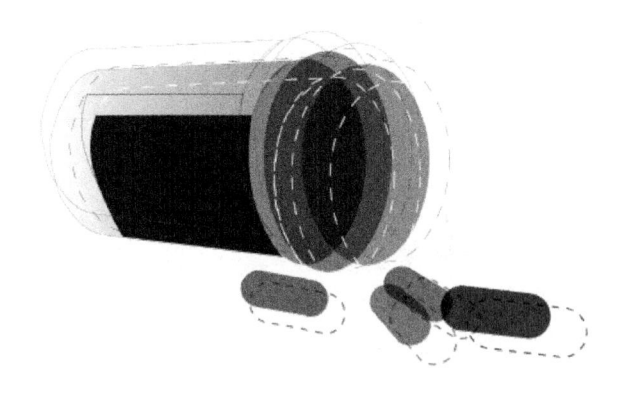

@oh_madeline_

**10/22/18**

    Our drives to school in the morning are my favourite way to start my day. I know it's cold out and we'd rather be in the bed cuddling, but I spend the whole drive admiring just how beautiful you are. I don't think you notice because you have to pay attention to the road. The way you sway your head to your favourite songs and hum softly to the beats in between the lyrics. When I say I admire every little thing you do, it's true. You won't notice just how bright my eyes shine for you right now, but one day you will.

It's cold outside,
let's go hide.

**You're My Happy Place**

My life has gotten brighter,
My shoulders feel lighter.

The world has become more clear,
I want to keep holding you, my dear.

I have fallen in a hole,
Their words have taken a toll.

Love isn't easy,
I don't mean to be cheesy.

**10/29/18**

    I take a lot of pictures of you. I like to look back at them and remember why you were smiling. It was probably something stupid that I said, but your smile has been something that lights up any room.

@oh_madeline_

Come fly with me,
Let the world be.

# I Like Your Face

Pure beauty,
Reminds me of a vine that's fruity.

Both scents that we hate,
But a bond our love will create.

I watch her fix herself in the mirror,
I can see everything clearer.

She's a perfectionist,
And sometimes the biggest pessimist.

When I look her way,
I forget what to say.

@oh_madeline_

**11/02/18**

    I wish our love could be picture perfect forever. I wish that you would always be happy with me, but I know how these things work. There comes an ending to every happy moment. I could be in denial all my life to think that this day would never come, but I know when to face reality. Things become difficult, communication worsens, we get annoyed by every little thing.

    We spent the last six months on vacation with each other. Sleepovers, parties, dinner dates, nights out, and lots of nights inside. We even explored a new country together.

    I pray our love can stay this strong forever.

I've always been one
to forget about the calm
before the storm.

# THE STORM

**I'm Scared**

It's time for more change,
I wish things wouldn't rearrange.

Turn the next page,
We must embrace a new rage.

I think it will all be okay,
But who am I to say?

@oh_madeline_

## 11/13/18

    I used to watch a lot of movies about ***love***. I hated them all. They were always so cliche… boy and girl meet, they fall in love, something, or someone comes in between, they fight, they spend a dramatic three days apart, realize they can't be without each other and run back to one another. There. I just wrote the beginning, middle, and end of a typical romance movie. My love life does not compare, for starters, it is way more dramatic and realistic.

Girl meets girl,
Broken girl falls in love with a lost girl.

Lost girl gets scared of real love,
Lost girl runs back to her past.

Broken girl hides behind a man,
Broken girl keeps running into lost girl.

Broken girl gets even more broken,
Lost girl becomes even more lost.

Eventually, their two found and fixed
souls pull each other closer.
Their bodies eventually give in.

They finish the battle,
They win the war.

Lost girl gets found,
Lost girl tries to fix the broken girl.

Lost girl realizes she was the one all
along,
She shouldn't have run.

Someone just as confused in this world
came along,
She was just trying to help.

She did more than 'help,'
She held, she healed, and she swung
around.

Girl meets girl,
Girls are both a mess.

The girls both need each other,
The girls hold onto each other.

The girls' love will continue to grow,
They planted everlasting seeds.

@oh_madeline_

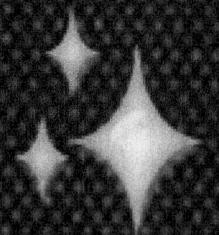

I wish you still saw me
with sparkles in your eyes.

**Red**

The anger has been growing,
I hate myself for knowing.

I dread this,
I want to feel bliss.

**The Love Story From The Start**

     So here is how it went. I was blindfolded and spun, forced to get through life. She came up to me, removed my blindfold and made me feel found. Before I could take a deep breath or enjoy the moment, I was forced back into the darkness. My manipulator ran circles in my mind, my saviour was trying to pull me from behind. I couldn't think, I couldn't see. My heart was racing, **let me be**. I couldn't rely on anyone because everyone seemed so out of reach. I wanted to be with her, but I was lost. She wanted to help me, but I kept pushing her off and then I would call her close. I was never like this. My mind was always clear. I let the fog surrounding my life seep in and pull me away. Then came the day. I picked myself up and I did what I wanted to do. I said goodbye.

Now here I am…
She saved me…
She waited for me…
She loves me.

> Hey, I don't mean to bother you, but I miss you... a lot.

> I miss you too.

> I hope you're okay.

> I know I will be. It doesn't have to be like this.

@oh_madeline_

**Before The Clouds Disappear**

There was one really bad day,
There was not much to say.

I asked if it was him or me,
I needed to be set free.

Your words pierced through me like a knife,
A day before, you were asking me to be your wife.

It was strange to hear,
It is now my biggest fear.

**11/17/18**

Because of you, it took her longer to feel confident.
Because of you, she fears that I will cheat.
Because of you, she doubts herself.
Because of you, she hides her hairs.
Because of you, she can't think for herself.
Because of you, she was hard to get through to.

But...

Because of me, she loves herself.
Because of me, she smiles longer.
Because of me, she doesn't have to worry anymore.
Because of me, she **knows** she is loved.
Because of me, she is treated like a queen.
Because of me, she knows her worth.
Because of me, there will never be another you to mistreat and cheat.

@oh_madeline_

Not to throw your name to shame,
But you are the one to blame.

**Sway With Me**

I watch you sway,
To the words that I say.

Your beauty strikes home,
Our future is full of the unknown.

I close my eyes,
My dreams help me realize.

Your face against the neon lights,
Makes me regret all of our fights.

@oh_madeline_

**11/24/18**

'I watched the sky change from black to blue.'

That sentence is a metaphor for my life. In reality, the sky changed and turned its brightest because of her.

Next to her,
    I feel my safest,
        I feel my most alive.

There is a whole world to explore and I couldn't imagine seeing it without her.

I may disappoint a lot of people or maybe a lot of people disappoint me.

No one likes to see someone on top and doing better. No one wants to see you happy. Maybe not no one, but the most envious. Those who feel the most jealous, those who are not truly happy, those who hide their faces from reality. Those are the ones who hate happiness and everything it will offer you.

**I Love You**
    I Love You
        I Love You
            I Love You
                I Love you
                    **I Love You.**

Can you feel my love whisper to you when you sleep so peacefully?

Can you hear my kind words singing you to sleep?

Does my face appear in your dreams when they turn dark and unclear?

Do you feel that you consume every thought that races through my brain?

You may think my love is a lie, but I cry every time you get up and leave.

@oh_madeline_

No one wants to be ignored,
we all hope to be adored.

# A

The waves were getting high,
I never want to say goodbye.

A day without you,
Is something I could never do.

Please stay close to me,
You are my key.

I'll swim to shore,
It's you I adore.

@oh_madeline_

I wanted to tell you that I had a dream about you. Well, about us. We were flying through the stars in the galaxy and at one point, you looked at me and told me that it doesn't matter where we are and that you'd always make me feel at home.

**11/28/18**

    I don't like feeling like I'm less of myself. I know that I have potential. I know that I do shine. I wish you could see that. I wish you could say more pretty words to me. I guess I'm expecting too much.

@oh_madeline_

**Why Is It So Hard To Be With Me?**

Forget the dark,
It's time for a new spark.

You electrify me,
I don't want you to let me be.

Kiss me longer,
My love for you is growing stronger.

Revive my soul,
You make me feel whole.

**12/03/18**

    I'm calling out for help. Can anyone hear me or have I gone mad? I doubt the path I choose to take because you make me feel like I am a mistake. I let this fire in my mind burn until it goes out, but who knows if that will ever happen. Why should I speak when I'm forced to be silent and have no say. If it's hurting me, I will speak.

    It is unlikely that we will be truly happy. Why? Because we won't let ourselves. We force ourselves to think that life is supposed to be dark and evil because it is the only time we feel, when all we feel is pain. Our minds block out our happy moments and replace them with all the hurt. We think we will find happiness by revisiting our past, but if we keep chasing our tails we won't get anywhere. Life can be whatever you want it to be. Happy, sad, boring, fun. It's all about what you make it. Cut loose of all that holds you back. Start your own fire that will never burn out.

@oh_madeline_

> Don't forget about me.

> I don't think I can.

> Yeah, you say that now.

**I Know I'm Amazing**

Don't mistake me for a fool,
I am certainly no mule.

I stomp my foot into the ground,
I was lost, but now I am found.

I was thrown out,
That's what I would write about.

I have taken charge,
My ego is large.

From the bottom to the top,
I will never stop.

@oh_madeline_

**12/05/18**

    I forgive and I can move on, but the pain will still follow. The anger will still creep up on me at the most inconvenient times. You can lean in to kiss me and I'd imagine you kissing someone else. I know it's messed up and I know I should take a step back, but I know where I belong and I know it's with you.

**Please Sing To Me**

Sing lovely words to me,
Move your body as free as can be.

You're a strong girl,
You make my mind twirl.

Walk me through all of my painful days,
Your kisses put me in a haze.

I forget about my past,
Our love, it will last.

@oh_madeline_

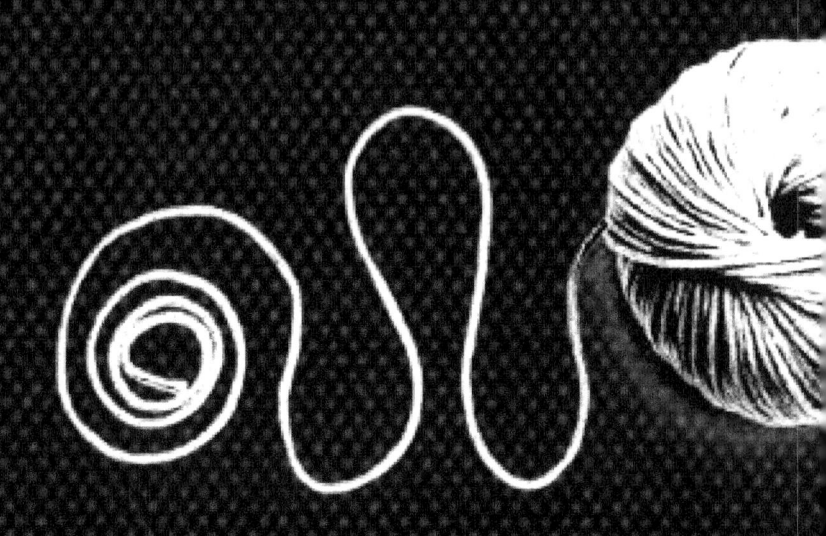

Sometimes we have to fall apart before we pull ourselves back together.

SECOND CHANCES

**12/15/18**

    There is still darkness in my life. I've learned to accept that it runs through my soul, but it is also what makes me feel whole. You're young, I am old, but we are both the same age. I took care of you for almost a year, now you rebel like you're going somewhere. Just like every parent, you learn how to let go and stop holding back. Eventually, they realize they need you and spend more time honouring you than fighting with you. This is all so strange to me, I've never experienced something like this. That's the point, isn't it? The unknown.

    I'm sorry I get so dark at times, I'm sorry if this has been placed onto you. I'm done making you feel sad, I just want to make you happy.

The shape of your face,
it feels like a comforting place.

**Please Stay**

Run with me,
Let's be free.

I want to see,
All that we can be.

**12/18/18**

    At first, I questioned the taste of your lips, the shape of your face, the way your arms felt wrapped around my body. I realized I've never felt at home before you.

@oh_madeline_

The taste of your lips,
match with your heavenly grips.

# Turn The Radio Louder

We listen to our favourite song,
I love when you sing along.

You're picture perfect,
What do you not get?

Stop hiding your smile,
I want you to stay a while.

We want this forever,
Don't say never.

@oh_madeline_

**12/20/18**

    The first night we met, my heart raced out of my chest and reflected onto yours. You couldn't keep your eyes off of me, but avoided any direct eye contact. I was mesmerized by your beauty, I still am. I spent that whole night absorbing who you are as a person and every detail on your face. Something about how unfamiliar you were to me, pulled me in and made me want to learn more. I drove home that night with the biggest smile on my face. You met me at a point in my life where everything was a mess. You continue to stick it out, as my life is changing for the better, you continue to support me in everything that I do and motivate me to want to keep getting better. As an individual who was so lost for almost all of my life, you've helped me grow in more ways than you know. So yes, our first kiss. What a different feeling, I didn't want to stop. It's like I missed your lips before I even got a taste of them. You are my one and only desire, thank you for starting this fire.

I won't let go of this,
You're someone I would always miss.

**Is This Paradise**

Through your eyes,
I realize…

It hurts my heart,
The thought of a depart.

I know I left before,
Please know ***you're*** the only one I adore.

"I will wait forever,
Just for us to be together."

There is nothing to fear,
I am here my dear.

**12/22/18**

    As time goes on, I think my favourite thing to do is ignore all that went wrong. I try to substitute the bad with the good, thinking it will overwrite all of the negative. When I know I've done something wrong to hurt the one I love, I'll break my back to make things right. It just sucks when it isn't reciprocated. I mean, who really wants to live their life in guilt?

@oh_madeline_

I wish I could be that piece of you,
you couldn't live without.

**No Need To Cry**

Pain consumed my soul,
I've almost never felt whole.

The sun never shined,
She's one of a kind.

These words flow,
I can never say no.

Your mind is full from the past,
I really hope this will last.

There was a time I sunk,
She removed me from that funk.

@oh_madeline_

**12/24/18**

    Looking at how far I've come and where I still need to get to overwhelms me, but the thought of knowing that you may be there with me throughout it all gives me peace of mind. I don't know how to really explain our love, I just know it used to be so electric.

I make it a habit
to look for the moon
every night because
it reminds me
of you.

**Practice Makes What?**

Spend your whole life trying,
Who will be there when you're dying?

There is a sad truth,
You'll even lose a tooth.

You can run away,
Or you can just stay.

We scare ourselves,
I've lived on shelves.

I want to be adored,
I'm sorry if you're bored.

**12/25/18**

    My journey with you has been an interesting one to say the least. We've had our ups and we've had our downs, but that's a whole part of getting used to each other. Before you, I lived in the unknown. I had no hope of anything positive. Fast forward past all the negative, we are here today. It's like we've fallen in love all over again and I couldn't be more excited. The world may not accept us together, but with my time apart from you, I felt nothing but emptiness. I've learned my lesson, you are my true blessing.

@oh_madeline_

I was told to stop
worrying about love
and focus on my passion,
but my passion wouldn't exist
if it wasn't for love.

**Circles Around You**

Read my writing,
These are the words I've been biting.

My mind is a maze,
Don't make me a phase.

I'm sorry if I scare you,
I don't really mean to.

I write when I'm sad,
I write when I'm glad.

It used to be all about pain,
Thankfully that's down the drain.

@oh_madeline_

**12/27/18**

I say I love you in many different ways:

    1)    I miss you
    2)    Be careful
    3)    See you soon
    4)    I hope you're okay
    5)    Drive safe
    6)    I can't wait to see you

I faced my fear,
I thought the end was near.

I thought you were going to go,
I didn't know.

I ran to you,
I knew you would run to me, too.

> I miss your voice.

> Me too, call me?

@oh_madeline_

**The Volume Is Too Low**

Switch the channels on my radio,
All I hear is the sound of your hello.

If I could sing,
It would be of all the love you bring.

There was silence at the start,
I wanted you to hear my beating heart.

The glass was shattered,
My paint was splattered.

Don't have anymore doubt,
There is no need to pout.

I am your song,
I've been here all along.

**01/01/19**

    I heard the birds chirping today. I mean it wasn't like it was the first time I've heard them chirp, but for some reason, they seemed louder. You were still sleeping next to me, but you didn't hear it. I realized at that moment, I wanted to be awakened by the birds chirping and the sight of your beautiful face every day.

@oh_madeline_

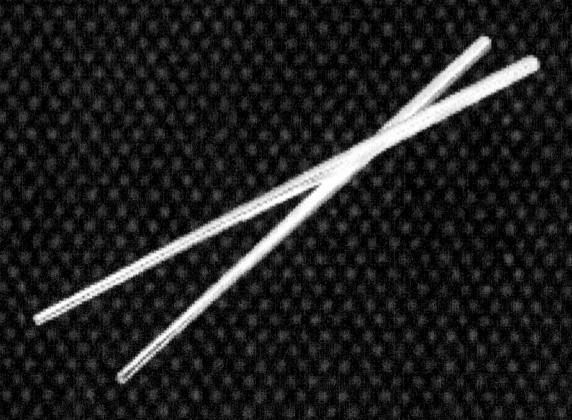

There is always room for two,
that's why I choose you.

**Flip The Page**

Scratch my soul,
I want to remain whole.

Our book's pages are still turning,
We are still learning.

I will fight for you,
Even when I don't need to.

Your voice is an ocean,
You soothe my body like lotion.

@oh_madeline_

**01/05/19**

    Would you care to read me? Like actually read me. Not just read halfway and then store me back on a shelf.

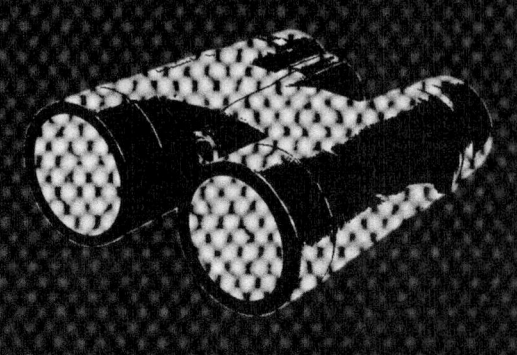

Don't come find me,
only if you need me.

**Just Love Me**

Stop treating me like shit,
What do you not get?

I'm here to love,
I won't put anyone else above.

I cry for you,
What else can I do?

When times get hard.
Don't play this card.

**10/10/19**

    I don't just overreact for no reason. I have a reason for every little thing I do. I used to run and hide from my problems, but now that I confront them, I don't always know how to. I'm learning along the way and I guess that's the best I can do.

@oh_madeline_

The mind plays games,

so why should we?

**Remember Those Times?**

Nights of laughter,
Towards our happily ever after.

I get lost in the bright lights,
I forget the meaning of all our fights.

I smile at you when you're not looking,
You're too busy with our next booking.

Wherever you want to go,
I'll be right by your side just so you know.

@oh_madeline_

**01/19/19**

    I feel like I'm too much for you. I'm sorry about that.

I wish I could fly.
I don't know where I would really go,
but I know I'd get there
faster.

**Like The Way You Used To**

Sitting next to you as you drive,
I've never felt so alive.

Playing our favourite songs,
Trying to sing along.

The radio is loud,
I feel like I'm in a cloud.

My hand clenched with yours,
This is everything I want to endure.

**Hello My Lover,**

    I'm just checking in to say that I love you very much. Things get messy, but with me is where you are meant to be. We will work it through like we always do. I look up to my ceiling, your face appears. I take the sign, so I wait for you to be mine.

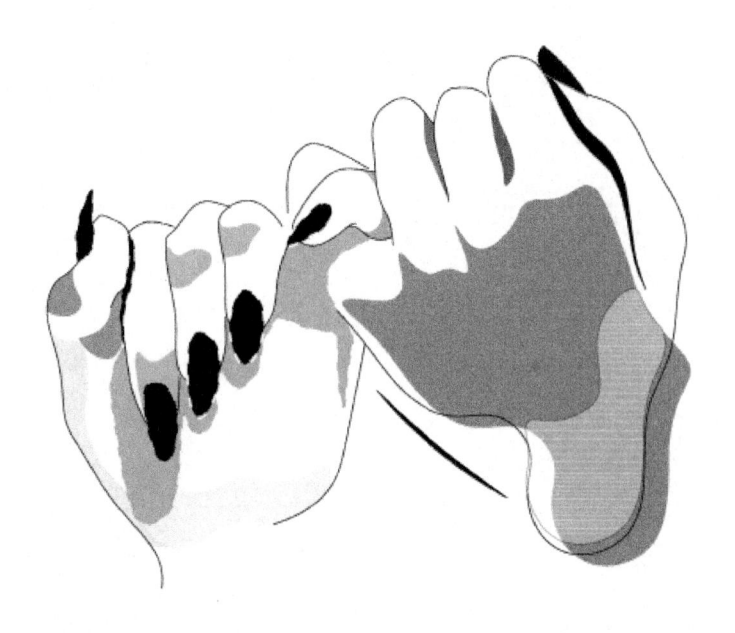

@oh_madeline_

I love watching the way
your face shines against
different lights.

# You Burn Like Fire: You Are My True Desire

Apples,
They don't fall far from the tree,
But what does that mean to me?

Plant your seed,
Watch me bleed.

I want you as a whole,
But there is a bite missing,
So come and take my soul.

@oh_madeline_

## 01/27/19

    Some say unconditional love doesn't exist; some say it does. I believe in it. I guess there's nothing wrong with her in my eyes. I'm not blinded by love, I can see clearly, but when you love someone, it doesn't matter if what everyone else says is right. You do what feels right. I know I'm not perfect, I know I have my flaws and I've made my mistakes. I'm still here with you, a year later, laying in the very same bed that made me feel so alone at one time. Now it feels like our own little home. We both hate to depart, but crave time apart. We rock the boat, but still manage to float. There is something about the chemistry between us; even when the world seems like a mess, we can both agree that it is at peace when it's just the two of us.

> I wish we could just run away from all of this and be together.

> It's not that easy.

@oh_madeline_

**Can You Hear Me?**

I call you from the street,
Am I yours to meet?

I catch your side eye,
The truth is, I couldn't lie.

You make me feel great,
I know you can't relate.

**02/02/19**

    I wish you would let me take more pictures of you. I love taking pictures of the most beautiful sights.

@oh_madeline_

To capture the essence
of someone else's beauty
is what I live for.

# I'll Catch You If You Fall

There was the crash,
Everything I knew gone within a flash.

I ran as fast as I could,
I wanted to make sure everything was good.

Everything was stopped in time,
I knew it would all be fine.

There I was, the only one next to you,
What happened to your crew?

You've never been adored,
So why do you feel so bored?

I show you my love,
That's why I place you above.

@oh_madeline_

**02/14/19**

    I'd run to you no matter where you were. The troubles that you may face, I want to be there for you. But most importantly, I want to be there **with you.**

We made a pinky promise to
stick by each other no matter what,
and I take pinky promises
very seriously.

**Slow Down**

You always want to run,
It seems like I am no longer any fun.

You say nothing makes you happy,
That makes me feel crappy.

You waited for me,
Now it is my turn to wait and see.

At the end of the day,
With me is where you stay.

**02/19/19**

    Sometimes I wish flipping a coin could give us all the answers we need.

@oh_madeline_

Heads or tails,

it never fails.

# Keep Shining Your Light On Me

Hey beautiful girl,
You make my head twirl.

I know you tell me to go,
But my response will always be no.

I am here to be your lover,
There is no other.

You are my sun,
I want you to have fun.

When you use a different tone,
Just know you aren't alone.

I am here,
Have I made myself clear?

@oh_madeline_

**02/24/19**

    I sit here in the sun, as it beams down on my face. I start to think back on all I wish I could erase. I realized these past traumas shouldn't linger this long. My subconscious is trying to overpower my conscious state.

Sometimes you have to remember to take a deep breath.

# The Air I Breathe

I'll sing my sad song,
As long as you sing along.

I'm mesmerized by your voice,
You are my only choice.

I inhale fire,
In hopes to be your one true desire.

**03/05/19**

    Do you think that the stars shine bright to remind us of all the pretty things that have yet to come?

@oh_madeline_

Always make a wish, but this time stop doubting that it will come true.

## It's Every Little Thing You Do

Your beautiful smile,
Makes me run that extra mile.

I'd do anything for you,
I know you would too.

I watch the way your eyes focus,
I believe in a world built for us.

I hope you see the changes,
I want to be here for ages.

@oh_madeline_

**03/16/19**

    I used to sit on the roof of my house a lot. The cars that would pass by wouldn't know what it was that I was doing up there. They often had concerned looks on their faces, but they never saw what it was that I saw. It was one of the most peaceful views. I got to see things from a new perspective and now that's something I try to do every day.

Not everything you see is what it's made out to be.

**Those Nights In The City**

We couldn't stop laughing,
Everything seemed so charming.

The sky was dark,
We were sitting in the park.

We were both so lost,
We needed time to defrost.

I always like to look at art with you,
I guess because everything feels so new.

**03/27/19**

    I have to stop trying so hard. I need to learn how to just be **me** and not a version of me that fits perfectly in everyone else's life. If my piece of the puzzle doesn't naturally fit with yours, then I have to branch off and find the ones that do.

@oh_madeline_

I am turning into the person
I am meant to be, I will attract those
who fit best with me.

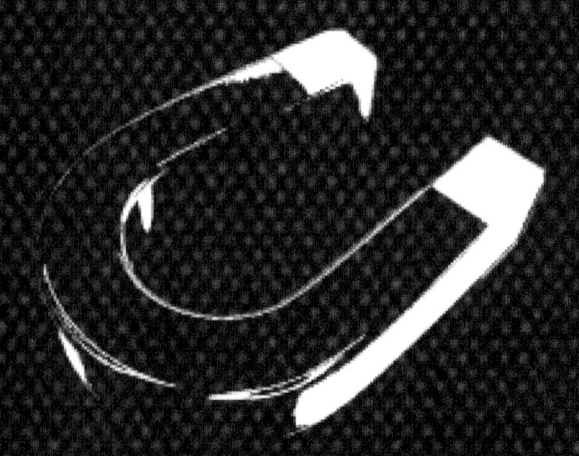

**Why Are You So Pretty?**

We went to go get posters,
Our memories may seem like blurs.

You were looking through the piles,
I was looking for your smile.

You're my kind of woman,
You are one in a million.

I can't keep my eyes off of you,
I wish you really knew.

@oh_madeline_

**04/14/19**

    I admire you the way you used to admire me. Are we going to keep chasing each other's tails or are we finally going to be at peace?

There was something about the way your kisses left me tonight. I know I kissed you many times before, but for some reason this time hit me like it was one of the first. I guess it might have something with you only wanting me at night-time.

**Believe Me, I'm Fighting For You**

I know it hurt,
But I will keep you alert.

I am here to love,
I will put no one else above.

I've slept beside you almost every night,
That safe feeling overpowers any fight.

You belong on T.V.
I'm so glad you chose me.

I'll make it worth your stay,
Just please don't run away.

**04/24/19**

Here are the times that I think of you:

1.  When I wake up
2.  When I'm getting ready
3.  When I'm driving
4.  When I get to work
5.  When I'm at work
6.  On my 5 minute breaks
7.  On my way home from work
8.  When I'm beside you
9.  Before I fall asleep
10. In my dreams

@oh_madeline_

Use me like you'd use an umbrella to stop the rain from ruining your hair.

**I'm Only Human With You**

We lay in the light,
Our future seems so bright.

We need to let go,
Of all we don't know.

Let's run away,
I know a place we can stay.

They want us to be apart,
So it's time we depart.

@oh_madeline_

**05/05/19**

The mind plays games on us all. I think I become the most lost when I'm left alone with my thoughts. That says something, does it not? I should probably figure that out.

Don't trap yourself
with your own thoughts.

**Baby**

Hold me tighter,
My world has gotten brighter.

You fill my soul,
I'm sorry if my love has taken a toll.

Your face is so lovely,
How did I get so lucky?

I want you to stay,
I promise I won't go away.

You've planted a seed inside of me,
I continue to grow like I am your
tree.

**05/18/19**

    I always try to lend a helping hand because I know that one day it will be given back to me. I've learned that the people I help, may not be the ones who help me back, but I hope that someone else will. I've learned the difference between lending a hand and getting stepped on like a doormat. Not many people like when they can't control you, so that's when they run for someone new.

@oh_madeline_

Water me like you water your plants, with love and care.

**I Can't Stop Looking At You**

There will be a happy ending,
My arms will always be lending.

I was a fool,
You always kept your cool.

I don't want to be a mistake,
I want to be yours without any break.

If you fall,
I'll be there through it all.

I have reached a new found glory,
As I continue to write this story.

@oh_madeline_

**05/21/19**

    I fall apart, I come undone, I get back up, I feel like my best self, and I fall apart again. I'm not the only one who follows this cycle. I mean we don't choose to follow it, it just kind of happens until we get tired of falling and we stop letting things knock us over.

Find a positive way
to view every crappy situation.

**As You Are**

Your face is glowing,
Our love is worth knowing.

I see it in your eyes,
You're no good at goodbyes.

Let's take a step back,
Why must we always attack?

We've both been hurt,
But I won't treat you like dirt.

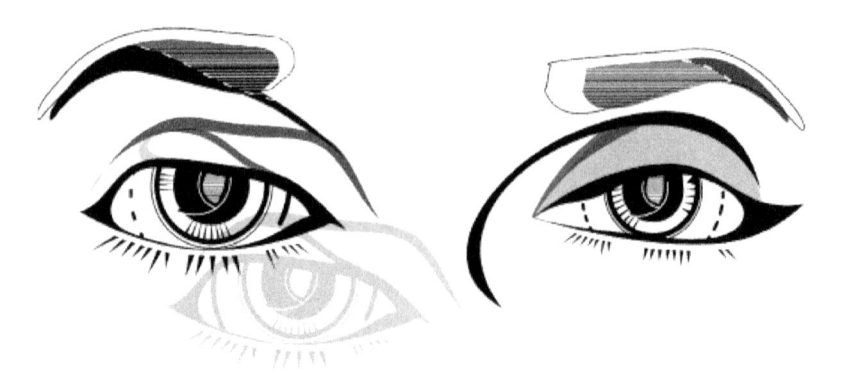

**05/25/19**

    I can't forget a face like yours. I mean I've spent almost every day memorizing where each beauty mark is or how far apart your eyes are and even the way your lips taste.

@oh_madeline_

> I hate texting, can we finish this conversation in person?

> Yes, I'm on my way.

**Step Forward**

Follow me,
Here is what I want you to see.

Don't stand too far,
I want you in control of my car.

I'd leave you the keys,
You don't even need to say please.

@oh_madeline_

**05/28/19**

    The last few months have been a few of my darkest. I've been trying to keep my cool for the sake of not making you upset. I know I am reaching my breaking point. I'm sorry.

I try to make myself the person that I would admire.

## Kiss Me Once More

Before you go,
I just want you to know,
That when the stars shine,
I feel realigned.

You make my nights feel like days,
You put me in a haze.

I went from a sight of black and grey,
To watching the waves along the bay.

So when you close your eyes to rest,
Just know you are the best.

**06/10/19**

    I hate all of the uncertainty. Are you coming back to me?

@oh_madeline_

Let go, grow, and go.

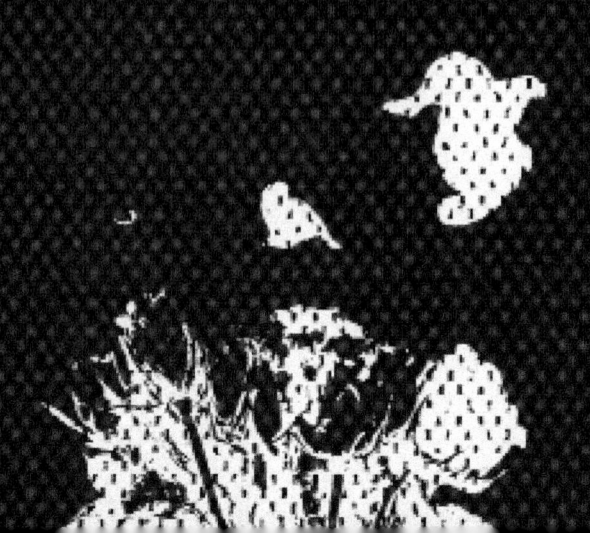

# THE GOODBYE

**You Fill My Sight**

My room is filled with you,
What a pretty view.

It hurts my heart,
When we are apart.

I'm sorry I'm not enough,
This world can get rough.

I want to fly,
Pain makes me want to die.

I'm only the most forward,
When standards are lowered.

**06/17/19**

    I learned to live every day like it is my last. I've watched too many people pass away and witnessed too many near-death experiences that made me learn the value of my life. I try to do something new every day, or well, as often as I can. I try to make a new memory, so that way I can say I have lived. I have to say you're one of my favourite memories, regardless of the bad. I'll always reminisce on the good.

@oh_madeline_

There is no need
to cry over the small things,
it wastes time.

**Done**

To finish,
To want to make a wish.

For a safe return,
From all that you learn.

To be free,
And climb a new tree.

It is the end,
Now there are things I need to tend.

@oh_madeline_

**06/29/19**

　　I think you reach a point where you see everything for what it is and just say "oh well." Until you get tired of saying "oh well" and you get up and make a change.

I am lost without you.
I don't know what to do.

## A Better Time For Us

You in a turtleneck,
A sight I cannot forget.

From the night we first met,
Smoking every last cigarette.

I craved you more than tobacco,
That's why it is so hard to let go.

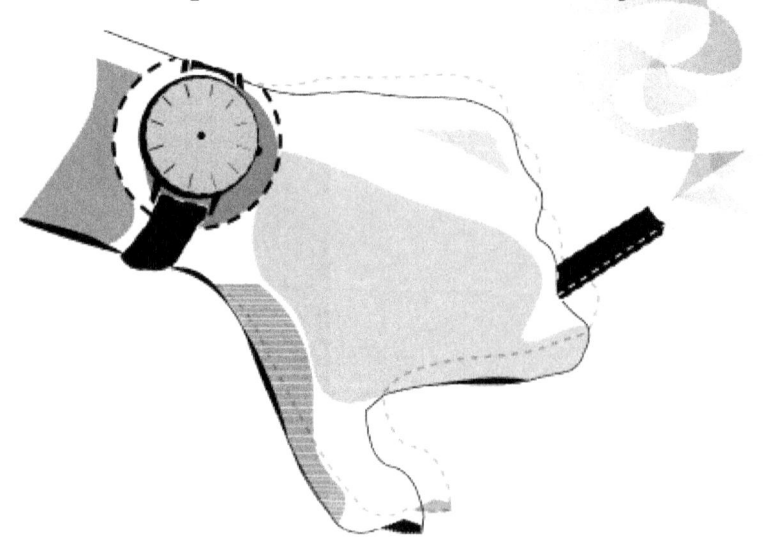

**07/01/19**

    I watch you clean through your closet. It reminds me of when we first started dating, as you pull out all the outfits you used to wear when I would take you out on dates. Fast forward to today, the day before you decide you want to leave me. I'm anxious because I know you're gonna leave and you're anxious because your clothes are a mess.

@oh_madeline_

You're the first person I want to tell everything to. This is going to take some getting used to, it's really hard trying not to bombard you. I've learned to accept this distance, but all I know is your face as the first thing I see when I wake up.

## Baby Come Back

I miss all the surprises I'd do for you,
And the ones you'd do for me too.

The love was so strong,
The timing was all wrong.

I hope that you're okay,
In another life, I wish you'd stay.

@oh_madeline_

**07/15/19**

    I guess I'll never understand how things can go from amazing to a mess so fast. I have a problem with letting go, maybe because of all the loved ones I've lost. When you don't fully 'recover' from something, it carries with you everywhere you turn.

    So when it comes to love, many people say it's not an on or off switch. But I've watched many of my past lovers shut me out and forget about me.

    How do you tell someone they are unforgettable, but even for the ten minutes you're away from them and with someone else, they can no longer mean anything?

You realized you were wrong,
with me is where you belong.

**Don't Give Up**

Take a wide turn,
There is still so much to learn.

I forget what it feels like to be in your arms,
I hate the sound of our alarms.

I miss how happy you used to be with me,
But I've accepted that I need to let you be.

**07/19/19**

    My overthinking mind; yes, it can be toxic, but look at all it has provided me with. I can think outside of the box because all I do is think and then overthink. Yes, many people might hate how indecisive I can be, but this is me. I must learn to be more direct and not afraid to speak my mind, but in order to do that, I need to be proud of every little thought I have. I have the ability to do great things, that's why I do them. I don't want to be in my forties regretting every chance I didn't take, so I take them all. I need to stop worrying about my past and look forward to the future, by living in the moment. Everything happens when it is supposed to. I have to stop controlling everyone else in my life and learn how to just control my own life. Here I go again, overthinking everything.

@oh_madeline_

> I wish you nothing but the best because you are my best.

> Thank you, you too.

**No More Us**

Why can it not just be me,
Am I not the ripest apple from the tree?

I am learning,
The world is still turning.

Why would I need another?
I already love her.

@oh_madeline_

**07/31/19**

The journey may have ended, but the new beginnings are in full effect.

Keep me sane,
You make me insane.

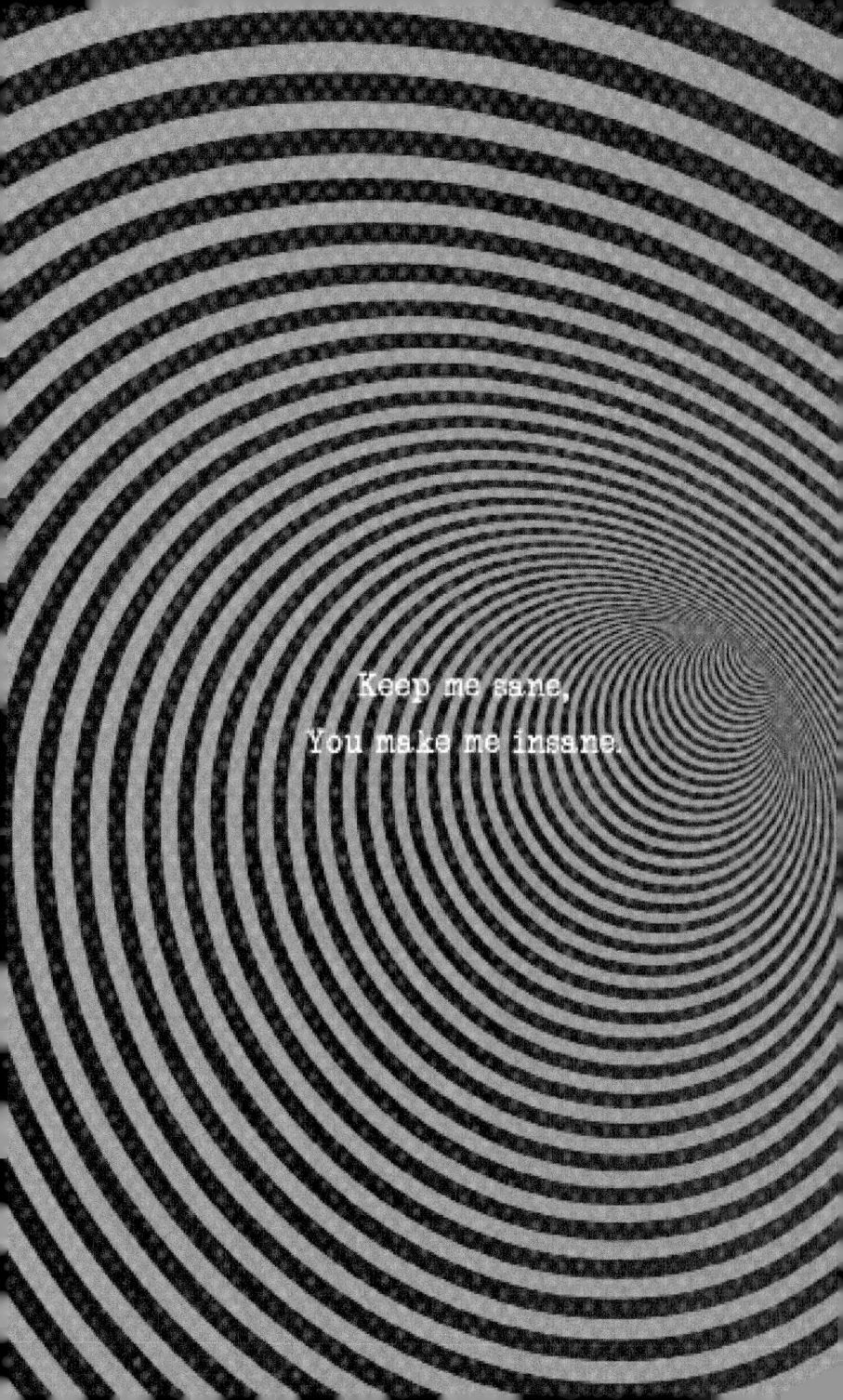

**My Assumptions**

One or the other,
You can't have both as a lover.

Now where do I go?
I feel so low.

Your decision seems to be made,
Now it's time I fade.

**08/01/19**

    The biggest thing for me is to never feel second best to anyone. I vowed to never let someone destroy me by comparing me to someone else. I guess a lot of things are easier said than done. We have to experience the worst before we reach our best.

@oh_madeline_

I write what I am passionate about,
that's why I write about you.

**Another Memory**

You'll forget about me,
You'll be able to roam free.

My loving heart,
Enough to tear us apart.

I was never the end goal,
So now I search for my soul.

I used to be your number one,
You used to be my rising sun.

Our love is never over,
For a while, everything will be a blur.

@oh_madeline_

**08/07/19**

    Here I lay in the soft light of the sunset, looking out for a sign. I wished for answers, but all that came was rain. As I was about to run inside, I began to realize how fast a pretty sight can vanish and how a new scene, with a new scent, can quickly approach without any warning. I sat there in the rain. Yes, I was soaking wet but the sky was showing me a new kind of beauty. At that moment, I learned how easy it is to run away when something turns ugly, but before you tie those laces, embrace it because you can never turn back time to relive it.

Eventually order will be restored, you have to be willing to wait.

**What Am I Suppose To Do?**

There will always be someone that comes in between,
Others love to intervene.

There is a beating pain,
Of the pictures that remain.

I've taken down my walls,
I dress in my overalls.

I guess it's time to move on,
I will no longer enjoy dawn.

**08/10/19**

    I could spend my life sitting here in self-pity or I could get back up and restart. Although we cannot control much, we choose how we can react to everything or how we let certain things affect us. It's hard to be positive in the moment. Especially when you've been surrounded by negativity and it is now all you know.

@oh_madeline_

There comes a point in any situation where you have to learn to go and stop forcing things to happen.

**Answer Me**

Do we love to feel complete?
Or do we love to compete?

Are we scared to be alone?
Or do we wish to find home?

@oh_madeline_

**08/15/19**

    I feel like a small pebble left at shore. Unsure if the waves will pick me up and take me to a new place, or if I'm supposed to be left here. The uncertainty of everything can kill, so how do we not let it? I guess we have to let go and stop caring so much. It's easier said than done. How do you lift yourself up when someone's stomping on you constantly? Find a moment to slip away and run.

It's over,
but it's never really over.

the end

**Okay, Stop Now**

I've been too negative,
Let's try to not relive.

Take a step forward,
Try not to make this awkward.

You need to grow,
I need to let go.

**Dear Lover,**

      Our time together has come to an end. We tried, we fought for each other, and then we parted. Will you still think of me as you go about your day? How I used to be the one standing in that spot, telling you how pretty you are. How about every time you go to tie your shoelaces. Will you picture how I used to do it for you? I lay on the side of the bed where you used to because it hurts more not seeing you there. I still jump out of bed in the middle of the night because I sense that something is missing on my end but on your end, you are complete. I must not dread this anymore, I have learned to let go. As much as I'd like to have control in my life, I've learned you can't control someone else's wants. Life happens and you learn from your mistakes.

Wherever it is written for me to be, is where I will be. My biggest fear is now a reality. I guess I've been preparing myself for this to happen. That stupid saying keeps repeating in my head, "when you love someone you have to let them go." I keep reminding myself that things will get better and I will get the love I deserve one day. I keep reminding myself that the one for me will no longer be someone who doesn't know if they want to be with me or not. I am deserving of the love I give. I am deserving.

@oh_madeline_

But thank you,

Thank you for all that you have done and for all the love you showed me when it was there. Thank you for the lessons you've taught me along the way. Thank you for showing me that I can be cared for. Thank you for showing me that I can't control everything in my life. Thank you for showing me that I am deserving of love and respect. Thank you for allowing me to give you my love. Thank you for calming me down all those times I let my mind overthink. Thank you.

If we ever meet again, I hope you are ready. Truly and fully ready to love, be loved, and grow. But if I never see you again, just know I am still cheering you on from the sidelines. I'm only a phone call away. I never meant any harm. I only ever tried to be better and do better.

I'm here. I'm always here.

Take care,

M.

Printed in Great Britain
by Amazon